Meditations

illustrations:
JAN GALLEHAWK

calligraphy:
JIM BILLINGSLEY

*if a man's mind
becomes pure,
so will his
surroundings...*

It matters not how
long you live
-but how well.

Pride makes us
do things well;
But it is Love
that makes us
do them to
perfection.

Some goals are
so worthy,

its glorious
even to fail.

We grow only
when we push
ourselves
beyond what
we already
know.

no one fails
when they
do their
best.

If a man cannot wait,
he cannot know the
right time to move.
If he cannot be still,
his actions will have
gathered no power.

From a quiet mind
comes vision;
From vision comes
knowledge of unity;
From knowledge
of unity comes
compassion for all.
From compassion
comes greatness.

Those who care
will be
cared for.

Ten thousand things
have their beginning,
In absolute
emptiness.

'Whoever uses
the spirit
that is within him
creatively
is an artist.'

'To make living
itself an art,

that is the goal.'

You don't get
to choose how
you're going
to die.
Or when.
You can only
decide how you're
going to Live.
Now.

*You make the world
with your own thoughts...*

The mystics say,
"Never judge a man
by his work,
- watch his pleasures..."

Life is not so
much what
each individual
makes of it,
but what we
make of it
for each other.

Helen Keller

Be good to you

Be yourself ~ truthfully.
Accept yourself ~ gratefully.
Value yourself ~ joyfully.
Forgive yourself ~ completely.
Treat yourself ~ generously.
Balance yourself ~ harmoniously.
Bless yourself ~ abundantly.
Trust yourself ~ confidently.
Love yourself ~ wholeheartedly.
Empower yourself ~ confidently.
Give yourself ~ enthusiastically.
Express yourself ~ radiantly.

The beginning
of wisdom
is being able to say,
"I don't know..."

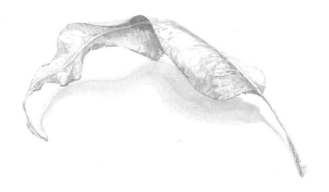

Ever has it been
that love knows
not it's own depth
until the hour
of separation

Kahlil Gibran

*Laughter is the sun
that drives winter
from the human face.*

Victor Hugo

You will know what you
are in time,
for consciousness evolves...

Thoughts lead on
to purposes;
purposes go forth
in action;
actions for habits;
habits decide character;
and character
fixes our destiny.

Tyron Edwards

Be good to yourself.
Be kind,
be patient,
be forgiving
After all,
you're all
you've got.

Become concerned
with complexity,
and you will lose sight
of simplicity.

*Give up winning
and losing
and then
find joy...*

When you see
the world
as part of
yourself,
you will take
care of it.

When you see
yourself
as part of
the world,
you will be
taken care of.

if there is a fate,
then it is fated
that we make
our own lives...

Everything that ever was,
is essential to what is.

The best reflections
are there—
when the wind,
water, and you
are quite
still.

Appearances come from
what is there;

Value comes from
what is not.

Regret little
-regret belongs
to the past.

a smile
is a light
in the window
of your face
that shows
that
your heart
is
at home.

Time moves not like a
river from here to there:
we do that. Time moves
in waves ~ it ebbs and
flows. There is a time
for everything.

The greatest value is not
in falling ~ but in rising
again when we do fall.

never fear shadows.
This simply means
there's a light
shining somewhere.

kindness is the
golden chain
by which
society is
bound
together.

An optimist
sees the rose;
and
pessimist
the thorn.

Hospitality
consists in
a little fire,
a little food
and an
immense
quiet.

We do not own
the earth.

Walk gently upon it,
so that future
generations may
do the same.

Water is the softest
thing on earth.
Yet its silken gentleness
will easily wear away
the hardest stone.

Happiness is a
butterfly which,
when pursued,
is always beyond
our grasp, but
which if you sit
down quietly,
may alight
upon you.

Nathanial Hawthorne

Complete quiet.
Energetically growing,
Restlessly changing,
All complete themselves
By returning
to stillness.

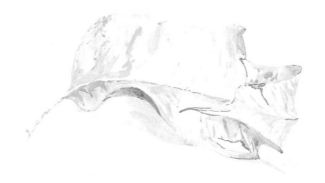

Others know more
than I will ever know,
Have more than I will
ever have,
Except for one thing.

There is hope
for anyone who
can look in a mirror
and laugh at
what they see.

You must make the effort to reach clarity or live life in a dream. Waking from the dream is hard—so be strict with yourself but never stern. Sometimes to put right a mistake only causes more errors —then it is better to pass on and remembering to forgive yourself. Punishment is not an end in itself—and the middle way is...golden.

Master yourself
~because it is fun...

Get away from life-lust,
from conceit, from ignorance,
and from distractions craze;
Sunder the bonds; so only
shalt thou come to utter
end of ill. Throw off the chain
of birth and death - thou
knowest what they mean
so free from craving, in this
life on earth.

Thou shalt go on thy way
calm and serene.

If you don't feel like
being pleasant, courteous
and kind, act that way
and the feelings will come.

Walls define the room;
windows, doors, and the
space within makes
it useful.

Of all loves the first love
is self ~ until you learn to
love yourself you cannot
learn to love another...

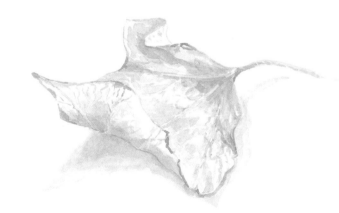

All journeys have a single purpose ~ to get to another place. There are places everywhere and the differences are less than you might think. Some places are no more than a state of mind.

'The way'
is a journey
-as long as
life itself.

Should enlightenment be easy? It is not! We have spent the whole of time that ever was, upon the way.

The blows of life transform us.

We are what we believe
and all that we are
springs from our own thoughts.

He who lacketh discrimination,
whose mind is unsteady and
whose heart is impure, never
reacheth the goal, but is born
again and again. But he who
hath discrimination, whose
mind is steady and whose heart
is pure, reacheth the goal,
and having reached it is
born no more.

If we live in peace
ourselves,
we in turn may
bring peace to others.

A peaceable man does more
good than a learned one.

Thomas A. Kempis

*happiness consists
in not having
many things,*

but in needing few.

All paths lead to the same end. All lives will lead to the same understanding.

Our perception of ourselves
is the only thing that prevents
us from higher achievements
~it either makes us
or breaks us.

A smile is a
wrinkle
that
shouldn't
be
removed.

There is a past
which is gone
forever,
but there is a future
which is still
our own.

The world is
a bridge, walk
across but build
no house
upon it...